DONALD ★ TRUMP ★

Biography for kids

INSPIRING STORY OF BUSINESS AND POLITICS FOR YOUNG READERS

BRIGHT FUTURE BOOKS

CONTENTS

Introduction

Have you ever heard the name Donald Trump? Maybe you've seen him on TV or heard people talk about him. Donald Trump is a person who has done many things— he's been a businessman, a TV star, and even the president of the United States! His story is full of big dreams, hard work, and lots of challenges, just like the stories of many famous people you may know. But what makes Donald Trump special? Why do people talk about him so much?

From building some of the tallest skyscrapers in the world to saying "You're fired!" on his TV show The Apprentice, Donald Trump has always found ways to stand out. He grew up in a busy part of New York City and, even as a kid, he dreamed of doing big things. He didn't always know he would be president one day, but he did know he wanted to be successful.

What does it mean to be successful? For Donald Trump, it meant working hard, never giving up, and always thinking of the next big idea. He faced plenty of obstacles and some tough times, but he learned that challenges can make you stronger and smarter. Through his story, we'll see how following your dreams, even when it's hard, can lead to some amazing things.

In this book, we'll learn about how Donald Trump went from being a kid with a lot of ideas to a businessman known around the world, a TV personality who made people laugh and think, and finally, to the president of the United States. Along the way, we'll see how he kept pushing forward, even when things got tough, and how he believed in himself and his dreams.

So get ready for an inspiring adventure through Donald Trump's life—a journey full of ambition, ideas, and dreams! This story shows us that no matter where we start, we can all reach for the stars and make a difference in the world.

Chapter 1

EARLY LIFE AND FAMILY

Donald Trump was born on June 14, 1946, in a place called Queens, New York. Imagine a big, busy city full of people, tall buildings, and noisy streets—this is where Donald grew up! Queens is one of New York City's five boroughs, and it's filled with people from all over the world, so there was always something exciting happening around Donald.

Donald's family was large, and he had four siblings—two brothers and two sisters. His father, Fred Trump, was a real estate developer. That means he built houses, apartments, and other buildings for people to live in. Fred Trump was very successful and hardworking, and he always had big plans for his business. Growing up, Donald watched his dad work hard every day, and this taught him how important it is to be determined and to go after your goals.

But Donald wasn't just interested in real estate—he was a kid with a lot of energy! In school, he could sometimes be a bit of a handful. His teachers would say he was smart but also a little too energetic. So, when he was around 13, his parents decided to send him to the New York Military Academy, a school with strict rules. They thought this would help Donald focus his energy and learn discipline, and it did! At the academy, he learned to work hard, follow rules, and become a strong leader. He also got to play sports, which he loved, especially baseball.

Donald's family also believed in something called "The American Dream." This is the idea that anyone, no matter where they come from, can work hard and become successful in the United States. His dad always told him that if he wanted something, he should go out and make it happen. These words would stay with Donald his whole life and inspire him to dream big, just like his father.

So, even as a young boy, Donald Trump was learning about hard work, discipline, and chasing big dreams. He didn't know it then, but these early lessons would help him one day make his own mark on history. His family, his schooling, and his love for competition would help shape him into the determined person he became.

Growing up in Queens, in the middle of a bustling city, with a big, hardworking family, young Donald learned that dreams can come true—but only if you're willing to put in the effort. And little did he know, he would go on to do some very big things!

Chapter 2

EDUCATION AND EARLY INTERESTS

When Donald Trump was sent to the New York Military Academy at age 13, he wasn't sure what to expect.

He quickly learned that this school was different from others—it had strict rules, uniforms, and lots of discipline! For Donald, it was like living in a place where everyone was focused on learning to be strong, determined, and responsible. He had to wake up early, keep his room tidy, and work hard every day, which helped him develop skills he'd use for the rest of his life.

At the military academy, Donald also found his love for competition. He played sports like soccer and baseball, and he enjoyed working with his teammates to win games. He even became the captain of his baseball team! Through sports, Donald learned that success often comes from practice, teamwork, and not giving up. These lessons about winning and losing would stick with him, helping him understand how to keep going even when things got tough.

After he finished at the military academy, Donald decided to go to college. He started at Fordham University in New York but soon transferred to the Wharton School at the University of Pennsylvania. Wharton is a school that's famous for teaching business, and Donald was excited to learn all about it. He studied hard, learning about money, real estate, and how businesses work. For Donald, Wharton was like a giant classroom for the world of business, and he soaked up everything he could.

While at Wharton, Donald spent time visiting his father's building projects. He saw how his father ran the business, managed workers, and designed buildings. Donald started to think about how he could follow in his father's footsteps but with his own twist. He dreamed of building huge skyscrapers and big projects that people all over the world would notice.

Donald's education was about more than just books—it was his first real step into the business world. At

Wharton, he learned the basics of finance and how to spot a good deal. And with his father's guidance, he began to understand what it took to make it in the real estate world. All of these experiences were setting the stage for Donald's future, giving him the tools he'd need to become a successful businessman.

So, even though he was still young, Donald was starting to see the big picture. His education and early experiences in business gave him the confidence to believe in his ideas and to dream big. He was getting ready to make his mark, and soon, the world would begin to notice Donald Trump's bold ideas and determination!

Chapter 3

STARTING IN REAL ESTATE

After finishing college, Donald Trump was ready to jump into the real estate world and work alongside his father. His father, Fred Trump, was already successful in real estate, especially in building homes and apartments in New York City. But Donald had even bigger dreams—he wanted to create buildings that would stand out, ones that everyone would recognize!

Donald's first projects weren't easy. One of his earliest challenges was turning an old, rundown hotel in New York City into something grand and beautiful. The building was in a prime spot, right in the middle of the city, but it needed a lot of work. Donald saw potential where others didn't, and he had a vision to transform this old hotel into something amazing. It took a lot of planning, hard work, and even convincing people to help fund his ideas. But Donald didn't give up—he stayed determined, believing that he could make his dream a reality.

With his unique vision, Donald took on more projects. He wanted to make a name for himself by building skyscrapers—tall buildings that would reach into the sky! Soon, Donald decided to work on something called Trump Tower. Trump Tower was different; it was a skyscraper in the heart of New York, with a luxurious design and shiny glass windows. When it was finished, it became one of the most famous buildings in the city! People were impressed by its height, design, and how it became a symbol of success.

But it wasn't always easy. Donald faced many challenges along the way, like finding enough money, working with construction crews, and handling unexpected problems with the buildings. Sometimes things didn't go as planned, but Donald had learned from his time in school and working with his dad that hard work and determination could help him overcome almost any obstacle. He kept pushing forward, and each building he finished became a new success story.

Donald's vision for transforming properties and creating iconic buildings helped him make a name for himself as a "real estate developer." This means he would take on big projects to design, build, and improve buildings that would leave a mark on the city. People started to recognize Donald's talent for creating amazing places to live and work, and he became well-known in the business world.

By following his dreams and staying determined, Donald Trump turned old, worn-down buildings into some of the most famous structures in New York. Through his hard work, he showed that even the biggest dreams can become reality with enough vision and effort. And that's how Donald Trump's journey in real estate began—by taking risks, believing in himself, and transforming ordinary buildings into extraordinary landmarks!

Chapter 4

BUILDING AN EMPIRE

Once Donald Trump had some real estate experience, he was ready to take on even bigger projects. He wanted to build not just buildings, but places that would be known around the world! Donald wasn't afraid to make bold choices or think outside the box. He had a vision for creating luxury buildings that would stand out in the crowded city of New York. And one of his biggest creations was Trump Tower.

Trump Tower wasn't just any building. Located on Fifth Avenue, one of the most famous streets in New York, it was designed to be tall, shiny, and full of luxury. With its sparkling glass windows and marble interiors, Trump Tower became a symbol of success and glamour. People were impressed by its unique design and high-end feel. It wasn't just a building; it was an experience, and everyone wanted to see it!

But Donald's dream didn't stop with Trump Tower. He went on to create hotels, golf courses, and casinos— places where people could stay, play, and relax. Each new project was grander than the last, and they all carried his famous name: Trump. He made sure that his buildings and hotels were stylish and eye-catching, with features that made them feel special and unique. Whether it was a luxury hotel in a big city or a golf course with a stunning view, Donald's projects became places people wanted to visit.

How did he succeed in such a competitive industry? Donald knew the power of branding. He realized that by putting his name on his buildings, he was making them recognizable. The "Trump" brand became known for luxury, success, and style. When people saw his name on a building, they expected something extraordinary. This bold decision to use his name was a big part of his success because it made his buildings stand out in a city full of skyscrapers.

Trump also took risks with his projects, choosing locations that others thought were too challenging or impossible to develop. He believed that with the right vision, he could turn any location into a landmark. Sometimes his bold choices led to big successes, and even when things didn't go as planned, he learned from the experience and kept moving forward.

Through all these projects, Donald Trump built an empire—a collection of buildings, hotels, and resorts that showed his unique style and determination. His bold decisions and commitment to luxury helped him succeed in a competitive industry, and his projects became famous around the world.

Today, when people see the name "Trump" on a building, they remember his story of taking chances, dreaming big, and creating an empire. His journey in real estate shows us that with creativity, confidence, and a willingness to take risks, we can build something amazing that lasts.

Chapter 5

TELEVISION AND CELEBRITY

As if building famous skyscrapers and luxury hotels wasn't enough, Donald Trump took on a new adventure—this time, on television! In 2004, Donald became the host of a popular TV show called The Apprentice. On this show, contestants from all over the country competed to prove they had what it took to work for Donald Trump. They faced tough business challenges, trying to impress him with their skills and ideas. And every week, Donald would decide who did the best and who wasn't quite ready, ending each episode with his famous line: "You're fired!"

The Apprentice quickly became a hit, and so did Donald. People loved watching him on TV because he was confident, charismatic (which means he had a magnetic personality), and always in control. He wore sharp suits, spoke with authority, and made big decisions with ease. Soon, everyone knew his name. People saw him not only as a businessman but as a TV star who made the business world look exciting and dramatic.

Being on TV wasn't just fun for Donald; it also helped him show millions of people what it takes to be successful in business. He taught contestants to stay confident, work hard, and think creatively. He also showed the importance of leadership—being able to make tough decisions, even if they weren't always popular. These were lessons that young and old viewers alike could learn from.

Donald's time on The Apprentice showed everyone that to succeed, you need more than just ideas—you need confidence, a strong presence, and the ability to communicate well. Whether it was speaking directly to the contestants or the millions watching at home, Donald knew how to hold people's attention. He taught people that believing in yourself and presenting your ideas boldly can make a big difference.

Through television, Donald Trump became a household name, famous far beyond the world of real estate. He had transformed himself into a celebrity, a personality who people would recognize instantly. And his message was clear: with confidence, charisma, and a big dream, you can make an impact.

So, from businessman to TV star, Donald Trump showed that sometimes success isn't just about what you know but about how you present yourself. His role on The Apprentice turned him into a symbol of ambition and self-belief, reminding viewers that they, too, could chase their dreams with the same energy and determination.

Chapter 6

RUNNING FOR PRESIDENT

After years of success in business and on TV, Donald Trump decided he wanted to do something even bigger—he wanted to become the President of the United States! Running for president is a huge decision because it means working hard, speaking to millions of people, and making big promises about how you'll help the country. In 2015, Donald announced his decision to run for president, surprising many people and capturing the world's attention.

Running for president wasn't easy. Donald had to travel across the country, speak to large crowds, and explain his ideas to the American people. He promised to make changes that would help people get more jobs and improve the economy. His campaign slogan, "Make America Great Again," became famous, and his red hats with this slogan were seen everywhere. Donald wanted to show people that he could bring his experience as a businessman to the job of being president.

His campaign was all about big goals. Donald wanted to improve the economy, secure the country's borders, and make changes in ways he believed would help everyone. He spoke with determination and confidence, telling people that he could bring new ideas to Washington, D.C. Donald's journey was filled with challenges, but he kept pushing forward, determined to make his vision a reality.

During his campaign, he participated in debates with other candidates, where he had to answer tough questions and defend his ideas. He had to explain why he thought he would make a good leader and show that he could handle the responsibility of running a country. Millions of people watched these debates, cheering for their favorite candidates and learning more about each one's goals.

In 2016, after months of hard work and dedication, Donald Trump won the presidential election. He became the 45th president of the United States, making history as one of the few people to go from being a business leader to becoming the country's leader. His victory showed that with determination, big dreams, and the support of others, anyone could aim for the highest office in the land.

For Donald Trump, running for president was a way to take on a new challenge and make a difference in a big way. His campaign was all about setting ambitious goals and believing in himself, even when others doubted him. By achieving his goal of becoming president, Donald Trump showed that dreams—no matter how big—can come true with hard work and determination.

Chapter 7

THE PRESIDENCY

When Donald Trump became the 45th President of the United States in 2016, he took on one of the biggest jobs in the world. Being president isn't easy—every day, you have to make important decisions that affect millions of people. For Donald, this was a chance to use his leadership skills and business experience to try and make changes he believed would help the country.

One of Donald's big goals as president was to improve the economy. He wanted to help create more jobs for Americans, so people could find work and support their families. He also wanted to cut certain taxes, which means people and businesses would have more money to spend and invest. By helping businesses grow, Donald hoped the country's economy would get stronger, giving more people a chance to succeed.

Another area he focused on was border security. Donald believed it was important to protect the country's borders, so he created new policies and worked on building a wall along the southern border of the United States. He wanted to make sure that people coming into the country followed the right process. His goal was to keep Americans safe and to make the country stronger.

But being president wasn't just about big goals; it was also about handling challenges. For example, Donald faced disagreements with other leaders and had to work with people who didn't always agree with him. He had to learn how to be resilient, which means staying strong even when things don't go your way. During his time in office, he learned that not every decision would be easy, and he sometimes faced criticism. But he kept working, determined to make a difference.

Donald's presidency also included important changes to healthcare and trade policies. He wanted to make healthcare more affordable for Americans and worked on creating new trade deals with other countries. These trade deals were meant to help American businesses by making sure they had fair rules when selling products to other countries.

One of the biggest challenges came during the final year of his presidency, when the world faced a global health crisis. The COVID-19 pandemic was a time when leaders around the world had to make difficult choices. Donald's administration worked to provide resources for doctors and hospitals, develop vaccines, and support businesses and families affected by the pandemic. It was a tough time, and Donald had to make many quick decisions to keep the country moving forward.

Through his time as president, Donald Trump showed that leadership means making tough choices and always thinking about what's best for the people. He learned that sometimes, leaders face challenges they didn't expect, and they have to adapt and keep going, no matter how hard it gets.

By leading the country, Donald Trump became an important figure in American history, showing that even someone from outside politics can make a big impact with determination and a strong vision. His story reminds us that leadership isn't just about the easy times—it's also about facing challenges and learning from every experience.

Chapter 8

LIFE AFTER THE PRESIDENCY

After his time as the 45th President of the United States, Donald Trump didn't just step back and relax. Instead, he stayed very active, continuing to work on projects and share his ideas. Just like in his business career, Donald believed in staying busy and always having a goal to work toward, no matter his age or status. His passion for making an impact didn't end when he left the White House.

One of Donald's biggest post-presidency goals has been to keep sharing his thoughts with his supporters. He continues to be a public figure, speaking at events, and rallying people around the causes he believes in. He shares his views on issues that are important to him, like the economy, security, and helping American businesses succeed. His dedication to these ideas has kept him in the spotlight and allowed him to keep influencing conversations across the country.

In addition to speaking to large audiences, Donald has also continued to work on his business projects. Whether it's his hotels, golf courses, or other ventures, he remains committed to growing his brand and sharing his passion for real estate. Even after being president, he finds ways to contribute, showing that there's always more to achieve if you're willing to work hard.

Donald's post-presidency life also shows that you can keep contributing and making a difference no matter what stage of life you're in. His energy and determination remind people that retirement isn't the only option; you can keep finding ways to make a positive impact. Donald continues to be involved in many activities, working to inspire others to stay active and engaged in what they love.

Through his life after the presidency, Donald Trump demonstrates that passion and dedication don't have an expiration date. His story teaches us that even when one chapter ends, there's always a new one waiting. By staying true to his ideas and working toward his goals,

Donald has shown that there are many ways to leave a lasting impact.

In the end, Donald Trump's journey—from businessman to TV star, to president, and beyond—reminds us that we can continue to dream big, no matter where life takes us. His life after the presidency shows that staying active, believing in yourself, and continuing to work toward your dreams can lead to new adventures, at any age!

Conclusion

LESSONS FROM DONALD TRUMP'S LIFE

Donald Trump's journey—from a young boy in Queens, New York, to a businessman, TV star, president, and beyond—teaches us some valuable lessons about dreaming big, working hard, and never giving up. Throughout his life, Donald faced challenges and exciting opportunities. By staying determined and believing in himself, he was able to turn his dreams into reality.

One of the biggest lessons we can learn from Donald Trump is the importance of determination. When he wanted to build skyscrapers or run for president, he didn't let obstacles stop him. Even when things got tough, he kept going, showing that determination can help us reach even the hardest goals.

Another lesson is resilience, which means bouncing back from challenges. Donald didn't always succeed on his first try, and he faced criticism along the way. But he didn't let that keep him down. Instead, he learned from each experience, used it to grow, and came back even stronger. Resilience reminds us that it's okay to face setbacks as long as we keep trying.

Confidence was also key to Donald's success. Whether he was on TV, giving speeches, or making decisions as president, he believed in his abilities and wasn't afraid to stand out. Confidence helped him lead, inspire others, and achieve his big goals. By believing in himself, he encouraged others to do the same.

And, of course, Donald's life shows us the importance of embracing big dreams. From his early days in the real estate business to his time in the White House, he always dreamed of doing big things. His story teaches us that with a creative mind and a strong work ethic, we can work toward any dream we have, no matter how big.

So, what can you learn from Donald Trump's life? Believe in yourself, work hard, and don't be afraid to dream big! His story is a reminder that with determination, resilience, and confidence, we can all make an impact and achieve amazing things. So go ahead, set your goals high, think creatively, and remember that your own journey can be full of incredible possibilities!

Made in United States
Orlando, FL
23 March 2025

59730322R00024